# SHARE

Twenty Seven Ways to Boost Your Social Media Experience, Build Trust and Attract Followers

Rob Anspach

Rob Anspach

# SHARE

## Twenty Seven Ways to Boost Your Social Media Experience, Build Trust and Attract Followers

**Finally**... a simple, easy to follow guide that shows you "real life" examples on how to improve your online communication to win over fans, friends and followers.

### Rob Anspach
www.robanspach.com

*"I'm impressed... love the cover... and your writing is very entertaining! I also appreciate the plugs for The Middle and BEN."*
**-Charlie McDermott, Founder, Business and Entrepreneur Network**

*"Rob knows his stuff! Sure, we are FB friends and I've been following him for a while. However, with tens of thousands of social media mavens out there, it can be difficult to know who to listen to, read and follow. Rob's tips and strategies are not simply re-hashed ideas you've heard a dozen times. He actually USES what he preaches and consistently ranks for the keywords he goes for. As a publisher myself, I'm generally more critical than others. In Rob's case, his book and deliverables are spot on. You'll appreciate his candor and integrity about what works and what doesn't. Most importantly, his advice is actionable and it works for anyone. You'll love this book!"*
**- Doug Crowe, Founder, Author Your Brand**

*"Rob Anspach demonstrates a key principle of social media marketing in the design of the book itself - the use of illustrations, photos, and screen captures. 90% of the information that comes to the human brain is visual. Anspach brilliantly leverages this to create an easy-to-read, easy-to-follow manual about social media marketing. What's really great about "Share" is how each of the 27 strategies can "stand alone" and the reader can read that chapter, log right into their favorite social site, implement that strategy, and get results. Buy and read this book and you immediately start to claim the power of social media as a business marketing tool!"*
**-Adam Hommey - Founder, Help My Website Sell™**

*"I absolutely hate twitter..why?...because I didn't understand it nor wanted to learn about it. This book helped me understand what I have been missing not working social media. If you feel stuck in marketing read this book you will not be sorry."*
**– Beverly Winter**

## SHARE

27 Ways To Boost Your Social Media Experience,
Build Trust and Attract Followers

Published by Anspach Media
P.O. Box 2
Conestoga PA 17516

Copyright ©2013 Rob Anspach
All rights reserved. No part of this book may be reproduced or transmitted in any form or by any means without the permission from the publisher.

ISBN 10: 0989466302
ISBN 13: 979-0-9894663-0-1

While they have made every effort to verify the information provided in this publication, neither the author nor the publisher assumes any responsibility for errors in, omissions from or different interpretation of the subject matter.

The information herein may be subject to varying laws and practices in different areas, states and countries. The reader assumes all responsibility for use of the information.

**Dedicated** to my wife and my kids for empowering me to write this, my parents for instilling in me the courage to never give up and to my best friend for always being there even when he was off saving the world.

This book is also dedicated to Bishop Joseph McFadden who died while I was editing this book. We shared many conversations via social media and I was lucky enough to travel along with him as a chaperone for the youth to Lourdes, France and World Youth Day in Madrid in 2011.

# Contents

| | |
|---|---|
| Introduction | 9 |
| Learn to Share | 11 |
| Share You | 14 |
| Share the Deeper You | 33 |
| Share Your Style | 57 |
| Share Your Entrepreneurialism | 76 |
| Just Share | 95 |
| Answers Shared | 107 |
| Acknowledgements | 113 |
| About the Author | 114 |
| Free Gifts | 115 |
| Speaking & Coaching | 116 |
| Recommended Resources | 117 |
| #Share27ways Photo Contest | 119 |

# Introduction

Social media has in essence become the new de-facto form of communication. We post, respond and message each other through our desktops and cellular devices...and yet, for most people, entrepreneurs especially, it's become a love or hate relationship of sorts.

In 2008 when I first discovered Facebook, I saw the potential in this social media channel to basically "up the ante" in my marketing to my customers. It was a fun new way to get people involved, to interact and get to know them a bit more.

Facebook was not the first social media network I had used, it's just they seemed to have simplified the process in a way that appealed to the masses. And, it was, at least for me, an easy to use system, that I used frequently and sometimes haphazardly to build my business.

Trust me on this...I made mistakes. Had my account frozen...twice! Yes, they are serious about those terms and conditions. And, had many people defriend me, block me and report me early on.

But, in light of violating the rules, and having friends ditch me...I discovered that social media opened up new worlds for me and expanded my business' reach far beyond my initial thinking.

So, I started writing about my adventures.

Hi, I'm Rob Anspach, an entrepreneur, who after five years of using social media discovered that everything that happens is a result of one thing...or should I say one word... "SHARE"!

Yep, this one word will in fact help you not only in the virtual world but has done wonders for me and other liked minded individuals in the real world.

In this book, you'll discover more about me and how this book can help you boost your social media experience, attract followers and generate more sales.

Now in case you're wondering what makes me an authority on social media and why I decided to write a book about it...well, I will tell you this... I've been speaking in front of groups, coaching entrepreneurs and writing about social media for several years now... and if you wish to succeed using social media you will have to...

# Learn To Share!

Look, the whole idea of sharing is foreign to some people, it's not that they can't share it's more like they don't want to.

I remember as a kid I wouldn't share my toys for fear that (1) I wouldn't see them again, (2) they would get broken or (3) get all dirtied up. Sure I was selfish... but they were my toys.

It's the same concept.

People are genuinely disinterested in sharing what they have with others. It's a fear. Fear of the unknown. Fear of the known. Heck, whatever the fear is...it's holding them back.

But here's what I've discovered that I'll graciously share with you...when you share without reservation, you get rewarded.

Maybe not right away...but, the sentiment will always be returned and usually increased in your favor.

It's sort of like tithing. You give a portion of your money to charity or church or wherever and in most cases you are blessed with abundance in return. Now, don't shake your head at me and tell me you don't believe in tithing, we all do it to some extent, some more than others and some not enough. But regardless, when you're done reading this book, at least you will understand the power of sharing.

So in order to help you increase your social media, or even your real-world experience I've broken this book into 27 different ways to share. Now there are probably a dozen more ways (some would argue a hundred more, maybe a thousand) but for simplicity I'll share with you just twenty seven.

I'll teach you how to share… how you use it, is entirely up to you. But, I will say this… being selfish doesn't build a business or win over friends.

## Learn the power of sharing!

# SHARE

… Rob Anspach

# Chapter 1

# Share <u>YOU</u>

# Share Your Story

## SHARE #1

*"No man can walk out on his own story!"- Rango*

Every one of us has a story to tell...and like most people, we enjoy listening to those stories. Is every story a good story? No! But, when we learn to tell our story, just like riding a bike, we become better at it the more we do it.

*A man lives on a farm, he writes to his son in prison - I can't grow potatoes this year. I'm too old to be digging up the field. Soon he gets a letter back from his son. You can't dig in the field, that's where I buried the bodies! The next morning the police came. They dug up the entire field but found nothing. Soon the farmer gets another letter from his son. Now Dad, you can grow potatoes. It was the best I could do from here.*

I love telling that story.

I bet you love a great story, don't you?

I know I do!

I remember as a kid, my parents would tell me stories of long lost relatives, and it intrigued me. I would fantasize about life so long ago.

I can picture in my mind the motorcycle accident my grandfather was involved in, which claimed the sight of his right eye. I was never there, in fact I wasn't even born when it occurred... but the stories I've been told... I can see it as it really happened.

Or, how my wife's grandfather would tell the story of how he came to America in the early 1950's from southern France to Pennsylvania with just fifty dollars in his pocket.

If you ever get to meet my friend Sal, he kind of looks like Emeril. He can hook you in with his stories, his life growing up in New York, and his experiences being a boxing coach...you just don't want him to stop. It's riveting.

I even get a "kick" out of my brother-in-law telling me about his karate adventures. It's all about storytelling!

I recently did an interview with Joe Sugarman for my "Passions to Profits" audio interview series. If you don't know who Joe is...well, besides being one of the foremost experts on copywriting, the guy responsible for launching BluBlocker sun glasses and author of many awe inspiring marketing & advertising books, he is also a master storyteller.

He would dramatize an offer to make it interesting and before long you felt like you needed whatever he had more than air itself.

Joe would weave stories about his experiences into his sales letters, advertising pieces and even his infomercials. Those stories would build drama, curiosity, fear or excitement. He would make you laugh or cry. He would get you involved and make you part of the story. And in the end, he would ask you to do something... buy the product!

Yep, a great storyteller can capture people's attention and get them to take action. And, in most cases that means added revenue.

Do you have a story to tell?

I bet you do!

I bet your story, how you became an entrepreneur is fascinating.

You should tell it.

> *"Your story may not have such a happy beginning, but that doesn't make you who you are, it is the rest of your story, who you choose to be...*
> *So, who are you?"* -Kung Fu Panda 2

In the social media world especially, most people don't know you or don't have a reason to trust you. Sharing your story will give them a reason to know more about you and trust you enough to either follow you or buy from you.

I'm curious...

- What makes you...YOU?
- What inspired you to start a business?
- How did you meet your spouse?
- What's with the nickname?
- How did you come up with your boat's name?
- How did you win that award?

**There's a story there! Learn to share it!**

# Share Your Experiences
## SHARE #2

In 1989, I ventured into what I thought would be an incredible business, only to watch in horror as it spun out of control and cost me thousands of dollars. It was one of those moments that defined me and pushed me to be a better entrepreneur.

It was roughly six years later that I started another business and like the first I had some troubles...but, I kept saying to myself, "I'm not a failure!" And, as much I tried to pump myself up...I was literally getting dragged under by my own shortfalls.

After three desperate years of struggling, I decided it was time...time to either get out...or get help. I choose the latter. I got help. In 1998, I flew to Arizona and participated in a business building and marketing seminar put on by a company called Piranha Marketing. It was gamble! I had no money, as the business drained it all. I was living on credit cards with no means to pay them back. I took to this seminar like it was my last meal...man oh, man...I devoured every last piece of information they gave me. Everything I learned was immediately put into action.

I credit that seminar for giving me the tools to help transform my business when I needed it. Back then, there was no social media, webpages were just in their infancy, there were no smart phones, no GPS and internet was powered by dial up. And yet, I survived and prospered.

That second business is now celebrating 18 years going strong and it gave the me the ability to have more freedom, more opportunities and yes, more fortune and glory...but it also gave me something else...knowledge!

And it's quite ironic because prior to being an entrepreneur I couldn't keep a job longer than a 1 year. I either quit or was laid off. I felt like the proverbial square peg in a round hole...I just didn't seem to fit into the role of an employee. Although, the term "attitude problem" was loosely used to describe me once or twice...maybe 4 or 5 times... possibly more. Not me? Nah!

What possessed me to start a carpet cleaning business was for a better lack of word kind of dumb. Sure I knew the technical side, but I had no clue how to market the business. And if I share with you anything in this book...marketing comes before anything in your business. And it needs to build trust.

It was October 1995, and I just put my stupid cap on and thought I was going to make a million dollars. And I would have if mistakes were rewarded at $10 apiece. I look back and wonder how the heck did I manage to pull 18 years out of this business?

I will tell you this...failure although disconcerting at times will provide you (sometimes very expensive) life lessons that can and will grant you the successes you seek. The key is to learn from your failures and not repeat them.

Or in my case repeat them often.

But it was through my carpet cleaning endeavors that lead me to learn to be a better marketer, a client retention expert, an author, a speaker and social media maven.

As an entrepreneur I discovered that learning from others experiences and sharing mine with them I was able to boost my business beyond my own horizons.

Without the ability or mindset to share I would still be banging my head trying to overcome all the dumb mistakes, sharing helped me leapfrog over all the learning curve crap and helped me be a better entrepreneur faster.

The fastest way to help another person get to know

you is share with them your experiences.

You'd be surprised at what you can learn from another person. Don't discount someone because of their age, how they dress or what they look like. I've learned some of the greatest wisdom from kids, ex-cons, or even passersby on the street.

When I was in Lourdes France in 2011 I was approached by a young girl, she couldn't have been any older than 12. She reached out to me and in the palm of her hand was a coin. I looked at her, she pointed to the coin. I didn't speak French, so I wasn't sure what she meant. My assumption, was that I had dropped a coin and she was handing it back to me, so I nodded my head in thanks, took the coin out of her hand and started walking.

I was way off on that one! Turns out that is how they beg for money and I just took a coin from a little girl. Well, after a kick in the shin and some donated coins I learned a lesson and gained nice traveling experience.

It's all about the experience...share it and let it be shared!

**What experiences can you share with another person that will enhance their life?**

# Share Your Past

## SHARE #3

In 1987 I was attending Penn State University and although registered as an Engineering Major I really had no clue what I wanted to do when I grew up. One thing was for sure writing would be a big part of what I wanted to do, but there was one drawback...I hated English. Not, knowing where to end punctuations or if I should put an exclamation point or a period, or where I should put the comma to break up a sentence wasn't my forte.

One day while in the cafeteria, a friend came up to me and asked what I was writing about, I said it was just a story. He asked what about. Oh, it's got girls in stilettos, gun fights and car chases what else is there? His eyes opened wide, and right away he pleads to read it. Reluctantly, I shared it with him.

He asks if he can show it to his English professor, I was hesitant, but my friend convinced me it was good. A few hours later my friend came running up to me and said I got an "A" from the teacher. I thought that's cool...considering I wasn't even taking an English class that semester.

I never did finish writing that story!

But I like sharing that story because usually your heart knows what it wants and it will fight your brain until the brain listens. My heart was leading me down the path of writing but my brain held me back for 23 years.

It wasn't until 2010 that my writing would take off and lead me finally in the direction my heart wanted me to go. I was asked to submit an article for Cleanfax Magazine, a magazine geared to the cleaning and restoration industry. So, I took it to task to craft a short piece that would help other cleaning entrepreneurs

Regardless of what industry you're in... I'd like to share the article with you so you have an idea of the power using the 3P's can have on your business.

### "Use the 3P's to create a dynamic business."

Companies who follow the 3P's are more productive, make more money, and deal with better clientele.

Mortgage companies, credit cards, banks and the insurance industry used to follow the 3P"s — and then they became complacent. The moment they stopped using the 3P"s, they found themselves in trouble... they got burned... and the government stepped in and bailed them out.

Most businesses (especially carpet cleaners) don't have the luxury of government backing, so not following the 3P's could cost you — big time!

What are these 3P's?

Prequalify... Prequantify... and Preapprove!

**Prequalify**

Is the client a right fit for your services? Not all are, and frankly, if you're not selective you could be putting undue pressure on your business.

When you don't prequalify, you are allowing *anyone* to use your services. You are not a "one size fits all." Learn to say "no" or tell the client you don't believe your service is the best fit for them and politely refer them to someone else.

To "prequalify" is to accept only a set group of individuals that meet a certain criteria. A perfect example is only marketing your service to the affluent or a certain profession (or both).

Most service-type businesses (especially carpet cleaners) have no mechanism in place to attract the right clientele. They put their ads in all kinds of places. They plaster every newspaper, magazine and billboard in their communities.

The problem is they don't have a clue who they should be marketing to, and when the phone rings, they don't "prequalify" the client to see if they are a right fit. They just book the job and hope for the best.

Are they in the right neighborhood? Is there parking available? How old is the carpet (or the upholstery)? When was the last time it was cleaned? Was protector applied? Are there any rips, tears or pulled seams? I'm sure you get the point, and you can set your own questioning parameters.

The more questions you ask, the better you understand the situation and the easier it is to "prequalify" the job.

**Prequantify**

Simply stated, is the job worth doing? Are all your costs factored into the quote?

If you're not making enough money to cover expenses then it's not worth doing.

There is no point being in business to lose money. Too many cleaners have in their mind that a lower price attracts more business. What it does is put you out of business faster.

How can you "prequantify" a job when you don't understand your true costs of doing business? What if, after factoring all your expenses, you realize you needed to charge *at least* $137 per job just to break even? Yet, your minimum service fee is $65. You are losing money.

Your minimum service fee needs to be at least 10 percent higher than the actual cost of doing business, and in this case $137 plus 10 percent = $150.70.

Will you lose some jobs? Probably. But, were the lost jobs worth doing to begin with? No. I have found that the majority of customers who were only looking for a cheap service rarely ever call back for additional work.

**Preapprove**

Does the client have the resources to pay you? You can prequalify and prequantify a client, but if they don't have the ability to pay, that's another story.

Make sure you have a payment mechanism for the services you perform.

It's always a good idea to ask for a credit card upfront to secure the booking appointment. This does two things. First, it tells the customer that your time is valuable and if they cancel the appointment without proper notice the card will be charged the minimum service fee. Second, you now have a back-up payment if their check bounces.

Here's the kicker. When you put the customer in control of payment options, it takes longer to get paid. Too many service companies still play it "old-school" and leave invoices and allow the customer time to pay.

What if they can't pay? What if they refuse to pay? What if they only partially pay? Or what if they pay and their check bounces? These are prime examples of why it's a good idea to "preapprove" and get a credit card upfront.

**Protection of the 3P's**

The moment you lift your guard and break the rule of the 3P's is the moment you allow the customer to take advantage of you.

It's when you allow yourself to get burned.

Instead of letting the customer take control, step up and use the 3P's to ensure you are getting top dollar for your services.

Since your future hasn't been written yet...all your best stories come from the past. Use the power of your past to make your future brighter.

Share those past moments (the good and the bad) to entertain, educate and engage others through your social media and real world interactions.

**What can you share from your past that will help your friends, fans and followers bond with you and get to know you better?**

# Share Your Passions
## SHARE #4

The one thing that most entrepreneurs possess is passion...it's that love for what they do that drives them, motivates them and pushes them forward everyday of their life.

In my audio interview series "Passions to Profits", I seek out those who exemplify passion for what they do and are willing to share those passions with others. At the end of this book I share with you how to get 4 of my "Passions to Profits" interviews for free.

My friend Steve Robison from Rehoboth Beach, Delaware describes himself as a left brain/right brain artist. He's a poet, a photographer, an author and a full time website developer. He has multiple passions, and he's always sharing them with others.

On the next page you'll discover one of his many poems he shared with his friends, fans and followers on Facebook.

**Steve Robison**

Silhouettes
Gradient approximations of life
Standing, posing, creating
A moment's view
At a slice, of brevity, of time
Between one curtain's opening, another's closing

The colors were her sustenance
The glimpses, her reason
The moments, the curtains, the rising and falling,
Her purpose

She set down her brush
Raised the glass to her lips
Tasted the depth, the red
Decided, this painting would wait
For some future
Undetermined
For some colors
As yet
Unrevealed

Last summer while camping with my son's Boy Scout troop at Cape Henlopen Delaware, I arranged with Steve to bring the troop to his office. While there, Steve graciously shared a few hours with them and taught them how to build a website. That's passion!

One of my Dad's friends has a collection of model trains in his basement. Not just a few, were talking hundreds...walls and walls of trains. His total basement has been transformed into a magical conductor's playground complete with bridges and tunnels and cities and lakes and, oh, you name it...it's probably there.

Some might called this a bit obsessive...but if you were given the opportunity to see his collection, you would understand the love and passion he has for these trains. The many stories he shares captivates those he allows to see his collection.

Without passion most people wouldn't have a reason to do what they do. There would be no model train collections, no book writers, no entrepreneurs, no poets, and no web designers...nope...all gone!

Without passion there is no "love of what you do".

Whether profit or hobby, explore your passions and learn to share them with others.

**What's your passion?**

**How can you share it with others?**

# Chapter 2

# Share the Deeper <u>YOU</u>

# Share Your Insight
## SHARE #5

My friend Lee Milteer, an Intuitive Business Coach, likes to share insights, words of wisdom and inspirational sayings. She takes what she's learned from her experiences as an author, coach and speaker and uses them in a way that provides others with fulfillment and guidance.

**Lee Milteer**

There comes a time in your life when you have to just let go of what is NOT WORKING for you. Things that bring you no joy, people who are low consciousness, agreements that people do not honor. Time to LOVE self enough to hit the reset button on your life. Release and let go of the old and reinvent yourself!

Sharing your insights with others is a powerful way to build your business without pushing a product or service. You are simply providing advice, or motivation of some kind, and allowing the reader to decide what action is required on their part.

It doesn't have to be a "rah-rah" speech, as Lee points out, sometimes it can just be a simple statement that has the biggest impact on someone's life.

Lee likes to help others reinvent themselves and teaches entrepreneurs to let go of the things don't bring them joy or inner peace, then shows them how to hit the reset button on their life to give them a new start.

Here are a few more examples I'd like to share with you...

**Chris Voss' Blog** @ChrisVossBlog
If you are not willing to risk the unusual, you will have to settle for the ordinary. Jim Rohn

**Kristina Korman**
Embrace life...Tell the people in your life that you love them and how much they mean to you..You never know when it is your last day.

If you're "short on sayings", that is, if you just don't know what to post to be inspirational, here are a few resources you can check out.

http://www.addicted2success.com

http://www.motivationalwellbeing.com/motivational-sayings.html

http://www.guideposts.org/inspiration/inspirational-quotes

http://www.inspirationalspark.com/inspirational-sayings-thoughts.html

If you feel inspired or moved in some odd way by what someone has shared with you, by all means reshare it with others.

**What insights can you share to help another?**

# Share Quotes

## SHARE #6

It's rather simple to do! And, your favorite quotes can be shared on Facebook, Twitter or the host of other social media networks. The question I always get is, "Where do you find quotes to share?" My answer is this... "I would first start with typing "quotes" in your web browser". The list will be endless, you just have to narrow down the ones that fit to what you wish to convey at the time.

Quotes from famous people seem to be the prevalent choice amongst posters, but don't forget you can also share quotes from movies, TV shows or other friends.

**Ron Shockley**
Weaknesses of attitude become weaknesses of character.~ Albert Einstein

**Meredith Bell** @MeredithMBell
"It is all one to me if a man comes from Sing Sing Prison or Harvard. We hire a man, not his history." - Henry Ford

**Lisa Birnesser**
"Even if you're on the right track, you'll get run over if you just sit there." - Will Rogers

Now if you'd like a few resources that will provide famous, not so famous and anonymous quotes that have been tagged and compiled, let me share with you these links.

http://www.facebookstatus123.com

http://www.quotationspage.com

http://quotelicious.com

Do you have a special saying that you use often? Why not quote yourself? Yes, you can do that!

*"The wheels a turning, but the hamster is dead"* is a phrase I would share with the scouts when I would see them standing around looking clueless. Okay, not very nice, but it got them to take action.

What's nice about quoting yourself, is when someone shares your quote with someone else and in return they share it. Then more people share it and before you know it... you're sort of famous.

Okay, maybe not...but it's always nice when it happens.

**What quote would you use right now to inspire, motivate or express gratitude to someone?**

# Share What Doesn't Work
## SHARE #7

> "I have not failed. I've just found 10,000 ways that won't work."
> — Thomas A. Edison

In 1989, at the age of 20, I started a video photography business in hopes of making lots of money. It didn't work! I didn't say "it failed"! I said it didn't work. Even though I had invested thousands into the business I didn't take into consideration I knew less than diddly-squat about marketing a business let along trying to run one.

Couple that with a partner who wanted to do things willy-nilly and who didn't adhere to the concept of established pricing.

The business lasted less than 6 months, but in that time I learned some very valuable life lessons. I discovered that having a partner without a partnership agreement was a dumb idea and that we were seldom on the same page with our thinking...and that we couldn't work together in any capacity.

I spent 6 years working odd jobs until I was ready

again to try my hand at being an entrepreneur. In 1995 I started a carpet cleaning business, a year later added a commercial janitorial service and by 1997 I had opened up a flooring store and thought everything was great. It wasn't!

I was expanding way too fast and overlooking mistakes that I thought I could fix along the way. Yes, sales were increasing every day, but so were the ways I found that weren't working for me. By 1999, I had had enough. The businesses were running my life…I was exhausted!

Something had to go! I needed to win back my life! Then I picked up a book called the "E-Myth" by Michael Gerber, and I discovered that I created my business to fund my personal life, and yet I was allowing my personal life to fund my business. So I did something about it.

I closed down the flooring store and cut back on some of the commercial nightly janitorial accounts to free up my personal time.

Some would've called what I did a costly failure; I call it another way that didn't work.

Doing what I did had some unforeseen consequences… more money!

By eliminating the services that were causing the most headaches, I ended up actually making more money not offering them. I no longer had the overhead, the expense or the extra labor required to keep those services running... so, I put the money towards something fun.

An eight day family vacation to Disney World!

*"All the adversity I've had in my life, all my troubles and obstacles have strengthened me... You may not realize it when it happens, but a kick in the teeth may be the best thing in the world for you."* – Walt Disney

The first time you are able to take your kids to Disney World is the moment when you realize everything you worked for as entrepreneur just came true.

Maybe it's the magic of Disney...who knows...but just seeing the excitement on my kid's faces...was priceless!

Sure, I got kicked in the teeth and had to overcome adversity, but I never considered not sharing my experiences because someone, somewhere might be able to learn from me and use what I've done to make their life better.

Sharing what doesn't work helps others beat the

learning curve.

Sure, sometimes overcoming your own obstacles in life gives you the knowledge to avoid future problems, but a helping hand with the insight to allow you to steer around the problems to begin with is a huge benefit.

Have you ever heard the expression, "fake it, till you make it"? Well, let me tell you, it only goes so far.

Confidence can be faked, knowledge can't.

*Go grab a pen and some paper... (yes, it's homework time!)*

- *List 10 ways that didn't work for you.*

- *List all the reasons why they didn't work.*

- *How were you able to overcome them?*

- *Who could you share this list with that would benefit the most?*

**Take the time to not only learn from others, but to share with others what doesn't work to help each succeed.**

# Share Your Friends
# SHARE #8

"The only way to have a friend is to be one." - Ralph Waldo Emerson

This one may be difficult for some! The notion of sharing one's friends with strangers isn't something that sounds easy. Some people are just very private and aren't accepting of people they don't know. Which if they use social media is kind of an oxymoron. Since social media is all about sharing, if you can't share… social media isn't for you.

As you'll see through this book I graciously share actual posts from my friends or companies I follow who I believe exemplify good social media skills.

When you "like" or comment on your friends post you are actually saying to everyone who follows you, I know this person and although we might not always agree I respect him/her.

I'd like to share a post with you if I may…this centers around my friend Nigel Worrall who owns a Florida vacation home rental company called Florida Leisure.

I've actually have only known Nigel for about four years, he was introduced to me by another friend on social media. Now I'm sharing him with you. Okay back to Nigel.

Now what sets Nigel apart from the rest of his competitors is that he does an excellent job of using video, social media and the power of the press to not only bring people to Florida but to rent his homes. I for one am a happy client who rented one of his vacation homes during Christmas 2010.

It was a huge 5 bedroom, 5 bath house with a game room, pool and jacuzzi in a beautiful gated community only a few minutes away from Disney World. And very clean! And cozy!

Anyway the post is about Nigel sharing his excitement when his company was recognized by the Walt Disney Company. Check it out.

And if you ever find yourself planning a trip to Florida look up Florida Leisure and tell Nigel I said Hi!

*Just a word of caution*...if going to Disney World or any other park in Florida during the Christmas holiday be patient and understanding as it's super crowded and ride wait times are very long. But the Spirit of Aloha Dinner at Disney's Polynesian Resort is simply amazing and worth the wait.

SHARE

**Nigel Worrall**
April 17 near Kissimmee, FL

Always nice when a company like Walt Disney recognizes your work and nice to get some good news today. We're part of the Walt Disney World Vacation Home Connection and we're subject to their housekeeping inspections. Our already good rating has improved further still... and we got brownie points as a result. Now all I have to do is figure out how to reward my housekeeping staff who have done an excellent job. A nice problem to have for a change!

Unlike · Comment · Share

You and 30 others like this.

**Rob Anspach** congrats! well deserved
April 17 at 9:14pm · Like · 👍 1

**Alberto Vazquez** Congratulations Nigel! It will be nice to see your properties offered when we make our next vacation plans on the Disney site.
April 17 at 11:06pm via mobile · Like

**Richard Sears** buy them wolverhampton season tix you should get them cheap no one whats to watch that rabble
April 17 at 11:12pm · Like

**Nigel Worrall** Hi Alberto... it would be nice if they featured us on their web site but just like their "Good Neighbor" hotels, we don't feature that way unfortunately. If you go to www.FloridaLeisureVacationHomes.com you'll see how we are allowed to promote our connection to them but nothing more than that.

**Orlando Vacation Homes, Orlando Vacation Rentals, Disney Vacation Homes**
www.floridaleisurevacationhomes.com
Orlando Vacation Homes for your Disney World vacation. Compare and Save your Orl... See More

April 18 at 7:35am · Like

**Nigel Worrall** I said "reward them" not punish them Rich.
April 18 at 7:36am · Like

**John Worrall** Great news, well done to you and your staff. Always great to get good news.
April 18 at 12:51pm · Like

# Share Religion
## SHARE #9

Yes, share your faith with others and you'll be surprised at how many people appreciate the thought and gesture behind it. To be honest I was a bit reluctant too! The idea of sharing my beliefs with others was overwhelming to say the least.

 Christopher West (Official)

"Worshipping God means learning to be with him, stripping away our hidden idols and placing him at the centre of our lives." - Pope Francis

But here's what I realized... if I can share my thoughts, my passions and my business with others, why can't I also share my religious convictions, because honestly, without religion in my life the other things wouldn't mean anything. So, I took a queue from others and started posting about my faith.

## *A few things happened...*

- *Conversations were started,*
- *Friendships strengthen,*
- *Beliefs shared,*
- *That overwhelming feeling was replaced with gladness and joy.*
- *And misconceptions dispelled.*

**Theresa Graham**

"Joshua told the people: Consecrate yourselves, for tomorrow the Lord will do amazing things among you." (Joshua 3:4).

**John Ramsey**

There are only two kinds of people: Can do people and can't do people! If you know Jesus, you have a mandate from God to Be Can Do!

**Father Larry Richards (Official)**

Do not be anxious about anything...by prayer and petition...present your requests to God" Phil 4:6 Give all your worries to Him

I've discovered more about other faiths in the last few years through sharing of my beliefs using social media than I ever thought I could. By sharing I was able to break down the barriers and start communicating.

Jacque Payne shared UMC Foundation's photo.

"Lego of your doubt, Peter..."

Matthew 14:22-33

Regardless of what religion you affiliate yourself with, posting about your beliefs helps you connect to those who share your deep devotion.

Except if you're an atheist, then sharing religion may not be such a benefit, but that doesn't mean you can't be nice to people offering up such a gesture.

On the plus side, if you don't know much about a particular religion and want to know more, chances are one of your social media friends can answer those questions and maybe dispel any misconceptions you might have.

**It's not about converting…it's about sharing!**

## Share Politics

# SHARE #10

*"I am neither bitter nor cynical but I do wish there was less immaturity in political thinking." - Franklin D. Roosevelt*

Back in 2009, I posted a comment that I thought was absolutely hilarious about the current administration...it backfired. A client saw my post called me on the phone, scolded me and proceeded to fire me. It was the first time I was fired due to my political beliefs.

But, I discovered that although I may upset a few people here and there with my political ramblings, the ones who stick around (who don't defriend me) will comment more and make having an online or even offline conversation more rewarding. No headaches, no getting scolded and no having clients fire me.

During the Presidential campaign of 2012, I along with half the nation were posting feverishly about the candidates we wanted to win and why. And, frankly it got out of hand. It was probably the first time since I signed on with Facebook in 2008 that I felt disgusted, aggravated and downright pissed off at how I allowed this medium to control my life.

It was to me and many others a tipping point...

information overload.

My wife "killed" her Facebook! She was tired of the drama and constantly arguing with so-called friends and had had enough. To her, not using Facebook was the best answer. To others, social media is as important as breathing, for them argument or not, they will continue to share their thoughts and feelings to others.

When it comes to politics it seems to be a love/hate relationship... and when the discussions get heated and they will... you'd better figure out a way to calm down.

 Bob Callahan

How does such an ignorant person become a congressman ??????

Don't we all ask that same question sometimes? And yes, some politicians do act a bit ignorant at times and seem to get themselves into trouble, but remember we (the people) elected them, we have the power to vote them out of office too.

Politics is one of those subjects (along with religion) that my grandfather once said were two things you should never bring up in conversation unless you were prepared to fight. Social media escalated those fights and turn friends against each other very quickly.

You're probably wondering why the heck would you post about something that causes all this drama, right? Well, the simple fact is, there are issues in this country that are of concern to many people and sometimes drama be damned, people want to feel they have a voice in what happens.

And, like religion, once I knew where my friends stood on certain issues I knew who would reply and who wouldn't before I even finished posting.

The Affordable Care Act (aka Obamacare), gun control and immigration reform are hot buttons in society today. But, politics also plays out on the local level and citizens want to know that their representatives are doing everything to protect them and their families.

On the plus side, I've discovered some new friends due to my political posts. Which is always welcomed.

 Michael Keller

As we all now know, we have some serious problems in our country. What can we do, as individual citizens to affect the rhetoric and the actions? Can we create a pocket of encouragement in our own sphere of influence?

**It's not about being a Democrat, Republican or Independent...it's about sharing!**

# Share Causes & Concerns

## SHARE #11

In the summer of 1999 my then 10 year old daughter was diagnosed with Type 1 (juvenile) diabetes. This was a crushing blow to me and wife emotionally, physically and spiritually. We felt like she was handed the death sentence. And, we desperately wanted answers.

For years we fought the doctors, we double checked everything they were doing and wondered if there was more we should be doing. We explored just about every option we could.

Naturopathy, acupuncture, homemade remedies... you name it, we probably looked into it. The stress of the doctors, the wrong insulin and fighting the insurance companies was overwhelming.

But as the years went by, and my daughter got older, we realized that although a horrible disease, it wasn't a death sentence at all, but it did have its moments. And, if my daughter's overnight hospital stays were awarded points like frequent fliers, she probably would qualify for a couple round trip tickets around the world.

As a parent of a diabetic child you are either proactive or reactive to the disease and how it effects and affects those around you. For the first decade my daughter would almost explode on people if they were making fun or even mentioned diabetes, they didn't know she had it...but boy, did she let them know.

My goal is to use some of the proceeds from this book to create a foundation that helps those affected with Type 1 diabetes live life to the fullest and gives them hope for a cure.

Speaking of foundations, that's what my friend did about 5 years ago.

It wasn't because her child had diabetes or any other disease...it was to preserve his memory and give hope to other families who suffered the loss of a loved one.

You see, while vacationing in the Outer Banks the Taylor family was involved in a tragic auto accident that claimed the life of their 3 year old son Drew. But instead of harboring hate and resentment, they turned the loss of their son into a memorial of healing for others.

Thus, the Drew Michael Taylor Foundation was born. And, the last several years this outstanding foundation has helped countless families by providing educational opportunities and grief and loss support programs for children, teens and their families.

**Drew Michael Taylor Foundation**
Spring 2013 event at Nancy Grayson Elementary School — Ready, Set, Go! early learning program

Or perhaps your cause is a little more personal in nature and centers around helping a local shelter.

**Holly Love**
Hey Lancaster Friends,
I am looking for a little help tomorrow around 3p.m. to help clean the Winter Shelter for Women and Children. The shelter closed officially today and will re-open in December. All of the beds and other supplies need to be moved to a warehouse... Anyone want to help, message me asap or if you have my cell text me!
Thanks in advance!

Whether you are looking for help to clean a Winter Shelter for Women and Children or participating in an early learning program sponsored by a nonprofit foundation... or raising money through a local Elks club to help a little girl recently diagnosed with Leukemia, share it with others.

**Rob Anspach**
April 23

...if you're in Lancaster County mark your calendar for this Sunday. This Elks breakfast benefit goes to help a 16 year old girl recently diagnosed with Leukemia. RSVP and let them know you want to help.

### PANCAKE BREAKFAST TO BENEFIT SARAH PARK

### THIS SUNDAY APRIL 28 8:00 AM - 1:00 PM

Sarah Park is a 16 year old Sophomore at Manheim Township High School who fell ill on March 31, 2013. She was taken to Hershey Medical Center for testing. On Monday evening, April 1, 2013 she was diagnosed with Acute Leukemia. She began Chemotherapy at Hershey Medical Center on Wednesday, April 3, 2013. She is an honor student, who also volunteers at the Heart of Lancaster. Sarah is an avid dancer at Encore Dance Center. Unfortunately, Sarah will not have the ability to participate in dance the remainder of the year or return to school this year.

The Lancaster Elks Lodge located at 219 North Duke Street Lancaster, PA 17601, is sponsoring a Pancake Breakfast to benefit Sarah Park on Sunday, April 28, 2013, beginning at 8:00 AM and ending at 1:00 PM. We are requesting a $10.00 donation for the breakfast. This event is open to the public. All proceeds will go to help defer expenses for Sarah. Sarah will also choose a Leukemia foundation to donate a portion of the money raised. If health permits Sarah would like to make an appearance at the event.

Parking is available off Cherry Street, as well as, the parking garage on Duke and Chestnut Street. RSVP to 717-397-7704

(As a member of BPOE #134 – Lancaster Elks – I shared the above post to help get the word out to make this benefit a success.)

Post what you care about, a charity in need or a cause that needs help. People love hearing about the good in things, so spread it around and share that good with others.

**If you know of a cause or concern in need...let others know too, share it!**

Rob Anspach

# Chapter 3

# Share Your Style

Rob Anspach

# Share Music
## SHARE #12

With sites such as Spotify, Meemix, Pandora, Maestro and Last.fm, just to name a few, sharing music with your friends, fans and followers couldn't be easier.

Since I grew up listening to classic rock-n-roll from the 60's, 70's and 80's these are typically the songs I want to hear when I search online services. My kids can't stand my choice of music... and they aren't shy about letting me know how old they think I am.

Songs from Queen, Aerosmith, Huey Lewis, Styx, Van Halen & Rush, not to mention the Beatles, Prince, The Monkees, Grateful Dead, Rush, Tom Petty and Genesis played a huge part in my high school years.

While I was attending Penn State and not sure of the direction of my life... "A Touch of Grey" by The Grateful Dead was the one song that inspired me to finish the semester I was struggling in and hang in there and "I will get by, I will survive".

When I hear the song "One Vision" by Queen I remember the summer I spent in San Diego with my best pal...we blared that song until we knew every single nuance of Freddie Mercury's voice, every beat and every guitar riff.

Two summers ago, I spent a few days at Camp Bashore helping out with my son's Boy Scout Troop. While dining in the mess hall one night the song "Juke Box Hero" by Foreigner started to play on the radio.

It didn't take more than the first two lines and every scout in the camp was singing along. Old & young it didn't matter...that one song brought us all together.

The point is... each one of us has special songs that mean something different. Maybe you remember the first song that played at your high school prom, or what was playing on the radio when you received your first kiss from your sweetheart. Every song is special.

Remember when music videos were actually played on MTV? My kids just look at me and wonder what the heck is MTV... they got YouTube! Yep, it's the ultimate resource for sharing your favorite music videos with your friends.

So, now when I really want to annoy my kids I share 80's music videos with them on their Facebook wall so all their friends can see how "cool" their dad really is... or not!

Ironically, my kids love listening to Weird Al which is at least for me an awesome way to bond. I mean really, who can't resist a song that parodies other songs.

Did you know...Weird Al's first aired comedy song was in 1976? Yep, and since then he has recorded over 150 parody and original songs. Just a little FYI... I didn't become a Weird Al fan until 1984.

Here's my Top 10 Weird Al song list...

1. Albuquerque
2. The Biggest Ball of Twine in Minnesota
3. White & Nerdy
4. Amish Paradise
5. Dare to be Stupid
6. Pretty Fly for a Rabbi
7. (This Song's Just) Six Words Long
8. Slim Creatures from Outer Space
9. Eat It
10. Ebay

Maybe Weird Al isn't your style, that's okay! Share what you like. Share your favorite song. Share your favorite singer. Share what makes them special to you.

**Share the music to connect with others!**

# Share Games

## SHARE #13

*"The score never interested me, only the game."* - Mae West

Back in the day, and still done in some larger cities, people meet up in parks to play checkers and chess. Yes, parks. That place that has trees, grass and swings. Social media has taken that concept to a whole new level. Now you don't have to venture out. You can stay bundled up in your pajamas and still feel connected to the world but in the comfort and safety of your own home.

I personally have blocked most games from my Facebook due to the overwhelming amount of time needed to play them. But I seem to get a dozen new requests every month from people who love to play games online.

As I was researching, that's my code (some would say excuse) for me being on Facebook. I noticed that with some of the new changes Facebook has been implementing lately, they now recommend games that you may be interested in checking out...regardless, if you have every single one blocked to date.

Not sure what to play? Well, if you're using

Facebook you can explore their App Center to narrow down your choices.

They have games like Mafia Wars, Poker and Farmville just to name few.

And, yes they can be addictive. But if you enjoy games, then have at it!

Most of the games rely on you to invite your friends to play. The more friends that play that particular game the better chance you have to move on to the next level.

But there's the kicker...some people will only use Facebook and other social networks to play games. They don't interact any other way...gaming is there escape.

Maybe you don't have a local park to go to play chess with a friend...online gaming brings your friend to you.

So, if you want to connect with someone and gaming is the only way...then pick a few games and enjoy the time with your friends. It just might make all the difference in someone's life!

And if you're like me who blocks most games, maybe unblock one or two for that friend in need!

**Share a game, create a memory!**

# Share TV Shows & Movies

## SHARE #14

When I was young I would watch reruns of Hogan's Heroes, Gomer Pyle, The Andy Griffith Show and I Love Lucy. In the 80's my favorite TV shows were MacGyver, The A-Team, Riptide, Hardcastle & McCormick, Airwolf and the Tales of the Gold Monkey, oh and I can't forget Cheers!

The 90's brought Seinfeld, Friends, Buffy, The Fresh Prince, Charmed, The X-Files, Star Trek the Next Generation, and my personal favorite Stargate SG-1.

In the last few years I've cut cable and went directly to streaming video through services like Amazon Prime, Netflix & Hulu. And with my Apple TV, I can mirror what I'm watching through network apps on my iPhone straight to my 42" flat screen TV.

The shows I've found through streaming that my wife and I enjoy include: Warehouse 13, Eureka, Numbers, NCIS, Psych, Primeval, and the short lived shows like Firefly, The Finder and Terra Nova.

Have I've seen Lost? Nope, can't say that I have and to be honest I've never watched Breaking Bad either, but all my friends talk about these shows...they share quotes from the show, impersonations and spoilers.

I just started watching the show "Arrow" based on the comic book Green Arrow, and I must say...I'm impressed. John Barrowman from the BBC show "Torchwood" plays Oliver Queen's best friends dad, who turns out to be not such a nice guy. But, I won't spoil it for you, you will just have to watch it and see for yourself.

In 2009, while celebrating our 20$^{th}$ Anniversary, my wife I and took a trip to California. There we toured Warner Brothers Studios and got to see the various sound stages where the TV show Chuck was produced.

It was at the time I noticed a poster for a new show being made at Warner Bros. called "The Middle". A comedy that airs on ABC.

A year later I interviewed Charlie McDermott for my "Passions to Profits" audio interview series who revealed to me his son Charlie was playing the role of "Axl Heck" in that TV show.

*That's my friend Charlie McDermott, his son Charlie (aka Axl) and me at a GKIC-Philly (now also called BEN, Business Entrepreneur Network) meeting in West Chester PA circa 2011*

Almost forgot to share with you some of my favorite movies and some of these have some really good one-liners that are great to share in quotes in your posts.

Here they are (in no particular order)... Highlander, Back to the Future, Commando, Princess Bride, Star Wars, Top Gun, Jaws, Predator, Alien, Indiana Jones, ET, Caddyshack, Forrest Gump, Blazing Saddles, Ferris Bueller, Heartbreak Ridge, Vacation, Ghostbusters & Animal House to name a few.

Can you guess which movie these phrases came from? (Answers below)

- "Hello. My name is Inigo Montoya. You killed my father. Prepare to die!"

- "You're all clear, kid! Now let's blow this thing and go home!"

- "Just a walk in the park, Kazansky."

- "Radiation suit? Of course. 'Cause of all the fallout from the atomic wars."

- "I don't believe it! Two barrels, and he's going down again!"

- "You have the manners of a goat. And you smell like a dung-heap! And you have no knowledge whatsoever of your potential!"

- "Human sacrifice, dogs and cats living together... mass hysteria!"

- "I'm making out a check for $1000, all you have to do is give me $300 in cash and keep the $700, all for doing nothing more than acting like a total creep."

**Got a favorite TV show? How about the latest movie you watched? Put it in a post and watch how fast people respond.**

(Answers: Princess Bride, Star Wars – A New Hope, Top Gun, Back to the Future, Jaws, Highlander, Ghostbusters & Vacation)

# Share the News & Weather

## SHARE #15

Did you hear the story about the news anchor who on his very first day on air got fired? Yep, he used a few choice words that I'm sure he'll never use again.

Bad news and horrible weather seem to fill our thoughts and we wonder what's next?

The devastation from Hurricane Sandy was crippling to some East Coast towns, especially in New York and parts of New Jersey. Thousands of flooded homes and cars that left people wondering the streets searching for food and clothing.

The Boston Marathon bombing was playing out while I was writing this book...and seemed to be on every TV channel and in the hearts and minds of those posting to social media.

News travels faster than light speed when powered by social media. It's incredible and surreal! People are now checking directly with their social networks for the weather and news and foregoing the televised reports.

In most cases, what your friends are sharing comes

directly from the local media.

**witfnews** @witfnews
Diocese: Heart attack caused Bishop McFadden's death - go.witf.org/kK2zv

**WGAL** @WGAL
Fire destroyed a vacant building Wednesday in Manheim Township, Lancaster County, that dates to the 1700s. on.wgal.com/17kqLSy

**The Patriot-News** @PatriotNews
Laptop computers stolen from Central Dauphin East High School: Police said the burglary occurred early Sunday ... bit.ly/15s0vbi

In the case of Bishop McFadden, his sudden death was a blow to the Diocese of Harrisburg. He was pronounced dead at 7:40 am on May 2, 2013. Within a few hours thousands of people from around the world had received the sad news via social media.

More and more people when they first wake up check what's happening on social media before they even get dressed, eat breakfast or even turn on the TV to see the news. Through our smartphones, tablets and computers we have access to all the world's information at our fingertips.

**What news could you share with another?**

**How could someone benefit knowing what the weather was like in your area?**

# Share Your Pictures

## SHARE #16

*"Every picture tells a story, don't it?"* – Rod Stewart

They say a picture is worth a thousand words, in the case of social media maybe more. Facebook, Twitter, Google +, LinkedIn, Pinterest & Instagram and the host of other social media outlets, have made sharing pictures a near instantaneous endeavor.

Pictures of flowers, animals, tricked out cars, vacation destinations, weddings, chocolate covered "whatever's", cartoons, sporting events, heck you name it...there's a picture for it.

When you share a picture you are connecting with someone on a visual level that in most cases doesn't need words to describe what the picture is all about.

Pictures are a way to connect with another person to share a moment in time or maybe even give an idea of what to eat or where your next vacation will be.

I recently returned to Arizona to attend an InfusionCon seminar and while there I made it a point to stop and see an old friend. His name...Tony Policci! The man responsible for inspiring me to learn marketing.

# SHARE

I hadn't seen Tony in over a dozen years, although we kept in touch through social media, texting and phone... on March 27, 2013 I got the privilege of hanging with Tony for a few hours. Very cool!

 Rob Anspach

...me and Anthony Policci at Jamba Juice in Chandler AZ (3/27/13). For those who don't know, Tony was the one who inspired me to learn marketing 15 years ago.

Yep, it was Tony who convinced me to attend the marketing seminar in 1998 that reshaped my struggling cleaning business and helped me to become a better entrepreneur.

**Every picture tells a story...share those story telling moments with others.**

# Share Your Check-In's

## SHARE #17

*"In this world of smartphones, the check-in feature is one of the newer, cooler applications -- it's not just about what we're doing, it's about where we are."*
- Kim Williamson

Foursquare, Facebook, Gowalla, Brightkite and others have radically changed how we share our lives through a feature called "check-in's". It's a way to inform your friends, fans and followers where you are or bring attention to a restaurant, theatre or place of interest for a chance meet up!

Unless you're Batman trying to keep your location secret... sharing your check-in's is a great way to interact with your friends. (And getting a compliment is an added bonus!)

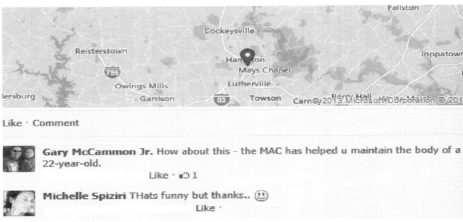

Checking in to airports or while in-flight gives your followers a chance to see where you're going or where you've been.

 **Fernando Cruz** checked in at Hartsfield-Jackson Atlanta International Airport (ATL) on Foursquare.
Home sweet home...

 **Mari Smith** checked in at American Airlines Flight 671 on Foursquare.
Whee -- greetings from 30,000 feet. I heart @gogo inflight wi-fi on @americanair! ;) (Let's see if I get that special badge. Hehee)

If you're a frequent traveler maybe you like to show off a bit by posting your exotic locales. Or, as Mari hinted at, that special badge that might be displayed with your check in.

Or perhaps you simply want to share with your

friends a great place to discover something really cool! Take for instance, when I go to my monthly Business and Entrepreneur Network (BEN) meeting in West Chester, PA I like to share that check-in with my followers in hopes that maybe a few will comment and want to learn more about what I do there.

Rob Anspach

The best place to discover smart marketing & business growth strategies — at Business & Entrepreneur Network B.E.N.

If you're an entrepreneur who wants to maximize the effectiveness of check-ins I would suggest creating a business profile. If you have fan page on Facebook, then in most cases you are able to receive check-ins, with the other services you will need to create separate profiles.

Once created you can offer special discounts to encourage first time check-ins and incentives for those who check-in frequently.

**Share check-ins and open the doors to your friends, fans and followers.**

# SHARE

# Chapter 4

# Share Your Entrepreneurialism

# SHARE

# Share Honors & Awards

# SHARE #18

 **Business & Entrepreneur Network B.E.N** shared a link.
January 24

The Power of the Press Release: BEN Member Rob Anspach, winner of the "That ONE Thing" Award, is generating buzz and garnering interview requests from a press release about his award...Congrats again, Rob!

Yes, I won an award! It was for a trust-based marketing piece I wrote that generated a 20 to 1 return on my investment in the first 48 hours. I wrote the letter as way to rebuild trust with past clients and keep my cleaning business going during the slow months. It paid off!

But then I did something crazy...a day after winning "That ONE Thing" Award I sent a press release out to various media outlets. The very next day I received a response from Cleanfax Magazine (a magazine for the cleaning industry) saying they wanted to run my story. Then a month later, Service Monster (a marketing & client retention solutions service for the cleaning industry) wanted to do a story for their blog...and a few weeks later Mikey's Board picked up the story and posted it to their cleaning industry bulletin board.

It was like winning that award over and over again. My friend commented that I was beating it to death…nah, I was simply maximizing the power of the press release.

Every time you share your honors or awards either through a press release or on social media you increase your chances of gaining additional exposure for your product, service, business, charity or whatever you are doing. The added exposure could mean more customers, more sales, added credibility or simply getting the word out.

In my case it was a bit of everything. I gained credibility, added more customers to my email database, got the word on what I accomplished and generated added sales.

As I was putting the finishing touches on this book, I again received another interview request to talk about the award I won and what impact it had on my business.

Yes, I was still getting interviews 6 months after winning. And, yes, it still felt awesome.

*"Rob, you are the master at getting the most from that award!"* – Charlie McDermott (founder of Business & Entrepreneur Network)

Yes, I am the master, but so are you!

You have the ability to do exactly what I did. It just takes a little effort. If you won an award...let others know! That's impressive!

There's nothing wrong with a little self promotion!

...I just won "The One Thing" Award at the Marketer of the Year Awards @ Business & Entrepreneur Network...for my marketing letter.

Use press releases to let the world know of your accomplishments and turn your one thing into an investment that pays dividends over and over.

**What honors, awards or accomplishments can you share with others?**

# Share Your Products & Services
## SHARE #19

When I attend networking meetings or meet people for the very first time, I usually get, "what do you do"? And, sometimes I give them my 30 second elevator speech. Other times I just make something up just to get a reaction. Don't laugh...it's a great way to break the ice!

Telling people you tame worms for a living or make art out of spent nuclear fuel rods really gets people to say "Wow, really? Tell me more!". I introduce myself then tell them the truth. Which usually leads to "oh".

Telling people you clean carpet and upholstery isn't a conversation that intrigues them. But, saying you are a "hero to busy moms" gets them to perk up and listen. Yes, a hero! Most of my clients are women and they have dirty carpet and upholstery so I provide a much needed service and save the day.

If you can cater your product or service to the right market using the right message you become a hero of sorts and people will seek you out.

"Be a welcome guest, not an unwelcomed pest" – Dan Kennedy

While attending InfusionCon (in Arizona - March 2013), I had the privilege of staying with friends. Now what makes their product unique is that it's man's best friend and companion. These beautiful Cavalier King Charles Spaniels are breed with the highest standards and care by Dulaney Cavaliers. These dogs are so tame I barely even knew they were there.

And, what's really neat about this company is once a year they have a reunion for all the dogs (and their owners, of course). They treat them like family... it's really heartwarming. It all goes back to passion, right?

 Dulaney Cavaliers

Sassy and the pups!

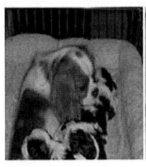  

The most effective way to get people to try your product or service is to make it something that doesn't feel like a product or service, that's not pitched at them or forced down their throat.

Take for instance my buddy Scott Seifferlein, who teaches the art of golf at the Watermark County Club in Grand Rapids Michigan. Scott is probably one of the best marketers when it comes to promoting golf instruction. And yet, he doesn't come across that way in most of his posts.

 Scott Seifferlein

Perfect night. Let's turn the lights on. I could teach forever in this weather. — at Watermark Country Club.

He uses social media as a means to communicate and showcase his services and not be an unwelcome pest to his friends, fans and followers.

<u>It's pen and paper time again...</u>

- o  Make a list of your products and services.
- o  What's your elevator speech?
- o  How do you break the ice?
- o  Can you describe in a compelling manner what you do in 10 words or less?
- o  Can you condense it down to 5 words or less?

**It's not about selling...it's about sharing!**

# Share Recommendations

## SHARE #20

This is one of the most powerful ways to build trust using social media...and Gardner's Mattress & More has it down to a science. In fact, they encourage their customers to share their experience through it. I'm talking about recommendations and why you need to share them.

**Robert Ford** recommends Gardner's Mattress & More.

Bought my bed from the guys about a year ago. I was referred by my chiropractor when I was having back and neck pain. Customer Service was incredible. I made 3 visits before making my purchase and Ben and his staff were very patient. If someone told me a year ago I was going to spend $2500 on a bed I would have said they were crazy. Now I look at it as one of the best investments I have made! I would refer these guys to anyone!

The recommendation box on Facebook only works if you have your business location filled out. Yes, the complete address. PO Boxes don't work. Must be a "real" physical brick & mortar location. Then you must click the little box below the address field that says, "Show this map on the page"...and bingo!

```
Recommendations

What do you like about this place?
```

You now have a recommendation box on your Facebook fanpage!

Encourage your customers to fill in the recommendation box... this does two things; (1)reinforces in those following you how great your company is and (2)shares with those following the person posting what they said about you.

Do you want to know how Gardner's Mattress & More maximizes the power of their recommendations? Sure you do! *(Just don't tell Ben or his staff I'm sharing this with you, okay... our little secret!)* They use screen capture to save the recommendation as a picture. Then they post the picture complete with photo, name and whatever saying to their website.

Now take it a step further and post the recommendation to your marketing pieces and host them on photo sharing websites. Think you can do that? I think you can!

**Who can you ask right now for a recommendation? Go!**

# Share Your Process
# SHARE #21

*"Don't worry about people stealing your ideas. If your ideas are any good, you'll have to ram them down people's throats."* – Howard Aiken

This one might be hard for some entrepreneurs to wrap their heads around. Share your process! What the heck does that mean anyway? It means share with your followers exactly how you do things. Look, understandably your fear of your competitors finding out what you do and how you do it is not something you relish, especially when it comes from your own posts.

But, for simplicity let's suppose you share a post with your followers that showed them exactly the steps you take to produce the product or service you're offering. That is a huge benefit for your clients and could be the turning point to convince someone to hire you.

In my carpet cleaning business I share with my clients exactly what my process is.

If you are not familiar with my service, here is information you need to know. The most important stuff...

- First, I vacuum your carpets using a commercial grade, upright vacuum. This will remove up to 60% of the dry soil, sand, grit and other particles BEFORE I start my cleaning process.

- I carefully diagnose any spotted areas and treat them accordingly.

- I apply a safe yet effective detergent formula to your carpets to break up the deep down soil and emulsify the grease, oils, spots and other particles in your carpet.

- Then I RINSE the soil, grease, oils and other particles from the carpet using a fresh, clean, pure water rinse. This insures that I remove all the dirt and detergents that are in the carpet.

- Then I groom the carpets to allow them to dry softer and faster.

Do some of my competitors do these? Probably!

But the simple fact is, it really doesn't matter if they do or don't...it's what my customers know I do that matters.

Sharing your process allows your customers to know exactly what to expect from your product or service.

It's about being open and transparent...it's about building trust!

**What's your process? Share it!**

# Share Your Videos
# SHARE #22

 **Jim Palmer - The Newsletter Guru**

*"Customers not only make buying decisions based on who they like (and obviously trust); they're also doing so based on who they have rapport with. In the online world nothing builds rapport like video." - Jim Palmer – The Newsletter Guru*

Yes, share your videos! No, I'm not talking about music videos, I shared that already. I'm talking about YOUR branded videos!

What you don't have any videos? You got to be kidding, right?

What if I'd shared with you an article I wrote that will have you making trust based videos with ease, and would give you added credibility and build rapport with your viewers would you make them then? Well, here's the article, then you can decide!

**The "little-known" and commonly overlooked elements to make your branded videos more effective!**

For several years you've been told about the power of making little video's and posting them to hosting servers like YouTube to build up your search ranking, back links and followers. But did you know, there is a magic formula to making these videos more effective and very few do it right?

Well, with the information I'm about to share with you, you just might want to invest in a personal video camera and a tripod. And, for less than $200 and the simple system I'm about to reveal, you'll have your online search ranking and customer acquisitions going through the roof.

No, it's not hype, its years of observing video content and seeing what produces and what doesn't.

And the simple fact is...it all comes down to 4 key elements.

Without these critical elements your video will not be an effective marketing tool...and you've wasted your time and maybe even pushed away your potential customer.

In far too many videos, I see the same method used to try to sell a product or service... "Hi I'm here to try to convince you to buy my product, so here it is, here's the number to call, buy, buy, buy, hurry!" This method is too pushy, too salesy and too downright desperate!

If you have videos like that, do yourself a favor right now and delete them.

If you want your videos to be warm and welcoming, to get your potential customer to call and comment you need to follow these 4 steps.

    I.    **Pose a question.**
    II.   **Introduce yourself.**
    III.  **Provide an answer to the question.**
    IV.  **Share your contact information.**

Here's how to put those 4 elements together for your next video...

(The below script was designed for a fictitious carpet cleaning company, but with some easy tweaking it could fit any industry and work just the same.)

"Do you want to know the secret in selecting the best carpet cleaner? The answer may surprise you! Hi, I'm Joe Dirt from XCEL Cleaning and I'd like to share with you that secret. You see, I've been cleaning for fine folks here in Little Town America for 18 years, and the best way to select a carpet cleaner, isn't over the phone. Oh, you might get a good deal over the phone, but honestly, when you invite a carpet cleaner into your home to perform an estimate, he/she now has a better idea of your true needs and can offer a solution that best fits your unique situation. Not all carpet cleaners are the same and some won't offer free in home estimates, but those that do normally deliver a more catered service. Why do I share this with you? Well if you're watching this you want to learn information that can help your situation and if you're in the Little Town area, I invite you to pick up the phone and call me. I answer cleaning questions like yours every single day and I welcome your call. You can reach me at 123-456-7890 or by email at yourname@yourcompany.com. Have a wonderful day!"

The script above is educational, non-salesy and very easy to duplicate. With each video, pose a single question and keep the video under 4 minutes in length. You don't need a production studio or need to spend countless hours editing it…just keep it simple and to the point. It may feel weird at first, but after a few times you'll get the hang of it and you're videos will improve. And with this simple formula you could easily come up with 50 to 100 questions that customers would want to know about your industry.

You can even use the videos to promote a referral partner, a vendor or even a product you love.

"Would you like to learn why we selected XYZ Company to host our event? Well, come on in and let me share with you this great information. Hi, I'm…"

It's that easy. One question, a simple straight forward answer and whamo, you have the magic formula for making effective videos.

By following these essential elements in your branded videos you will increase traffic on the major search engines while keeping the phone ringing with customers eager to hire you.

Now go make some videos, and share them with others through your social media and real world connections.

Don't know what questions to use? I would start with the common questions people ask you in regards to your business. Make a list...then script it out.

Like I said, I doesn't have to be an expensive production or fancy editing...it's about getting your message out there so people can discover who you are and how you can help them.

To repeat what Jim Palmer shared in his post... *"In the online world nothing builds rapport like video."*

Turn a question a day into a video and within one year you'll have 365 ways to build trust and rapport with your fans, friends and followers.

**Build trust by sharing videos!**

# Share Your Marketing

## SHARE #23

Now you're probably wondering why I have "share your marketing" almost at the end of the book, well, there's a good reason.

You see on social media and yes, even the real world it's a good idea to build trust first. I might have mentioned that once or twice before. Constantly bombarding your friends, fans & followers with your marketing message is a good way to lose them.

Sure, we undoubtedly want to attract people and get them to try our business or continue as happy clients…but we don't want to appear to them as desperate and pushy.

A good rule of thumb is to limit the sharing of your marketing message to about 20% of your overall postings. Some would argue 20% is even too much.  So, that's exactly why this book was written, to share with people additional ways to grow your social media experience without looking like a "pushy" marketer.

I love marketing, don't get me wrong. And, you

might have heard the more marketing "touches" we deliver the better chance your prospective audience will see your message...and that's true to an extent. But, social media is about being social so if you aren't prepared to Share #'s 1-27 when you try to use #23 (Marketing) it will backfire.

Create awareness for your brand, product or service by creating small talk first. Your fans, followers and friends need to feel romanced before being sold on commitment. So, start off slow, let them get to know you, trust you, then share with them your marketing.

My friend Gerry Oginski is a medical malpractice attorney practicing in the state of New York and he's a big believer in sharing his marketing.

**Gerry Oginski**

Being interviewed tomorrow 6:30PM @BronxnetTV CH67 Fios CH33 @DavidLesch on #nursinghome #liability w/ Michael Feldman #medical #malpractice w/ @GerryOginski. Join us for some great educational info.

As you can see from his post he's not "in your face" with a "buy-from-me" agenda. He shares with people where they can hear about his upcoming interview and that it centers around nursing home liability and medical malpractice.

I'm a big believer in "market your marketing", which is another term from sharing your marketing. It's a great way to share with your social media network the marketing you're conducting in the offline world (the real world). Just remember the 20% rule.

- Do you have monthly newsletter?
- How about a radio spot?
- Maybe a newspaper advertisement?
- A Val-Pak, Clipper or Yellow Page Coupon?
- How about a postcard or consumer's guide?
- Press releases?

Now take all those and couple them with what you might be doing on the internet...

- Website
- Blog
- Article Submissions
- Video

When you share your marketing with your fans, friends and followers, they in turn will share it with their network, who in turn will share it, and so on and so forth. Sharing your marketing creates brand awareness for your business, more customers and more money in the bank.

**Create awareness...share your marketing!**

SHARE

# Chapter 5

# Just Share

SHARE

# Share A Link (or a #Hashtag)

# SHARE #24

Sharing a link is probably the easiest way to drive someone to your website, a resource page, a production or maybe even a restaurant you would want them to check out. Maybe, you've noticed how I shared links throughout this book. It's the same way you should share links through your social media.

 **Rob Anspach** @robanspach
My answer to How do I increase the social media presence of a client in three months or less? qr.ae/TLfRb

Some social media sites will actually expand the link you share and give a brief blurb and/or picture to give the reader a teaser of sorts to engage them to click.

 **Premiere Carpet Cleaners** shared a link.

...discover the answers to common carpet cleaning questions.
http://www.premierecarpetcleaners.com/questions/

**Common Carpet Cleaning Questions and Answers**
www.premierecarpetcleaners.com

How often should you have your carpet, furniture, area rugs & mattresses cleaned? Discover the answer along with

# SHARE

Sharing a #hashtag (the number sign followed by some keyword or phrase) is a cool way to get people to interact and follow.

Hashtags have been around for numerous years, mostly on Twitter, but are seeing an increased usage across most social platforms. This is due to savvy entrepreneurs maximizing the power of keywords in their marketing.

Here I use hashtags to promote my cleaning company on Twitter.

**Premiere Cleaners** @premiereclean
...redefining service! #carpetcleaning #cleanguaranteed

Below are two examples using the hashtag **#cleanfax** to promote articles which appeared in Cleanfax Magazine.

**Jeff Cross** @Cleanfaxmag
Breaking news from #Cleanfax: The IICRC Certification Council is now voting. Asking the Education Committee to... fb.me/FpS6igvF

**Hydro Lab** @hydro_lab
"Hoarders" are helping the restoration & cleaning industry, which can bring in anywhere from $5,000-$40,000. #cleanfax bit.ly/LXwMvM

Got bed bugs? Well, my friend Scott "P Buggy" Linde

can help you get rid of them. Not only is Scott a successful pest control operator in Edison NJ, but also the author of two bed bug books; "Bite Back" and the new "Bite Back II - Confessions of a Bed Bug Killer".

**Scotty_BedBug** @ScottLinde
#bedbugs got you down? No fear, its coming to the market, check out this #pic #pestplus pic.twitter.com/GMc6ZDEryc

Scott uses hashtags and links in the above post to inform and make aware to his list of friends that his newest book will be coming to market.

What do you think? Easy, huh? It can be. Although, a good rule of thumb to remember is limit a post to one link and at most three hashtags. Anymore than one link or three hashtags and it gets distracting, cluttered and comes off as a "pushy sales" post.

If you have a product or service, there is probably a hashtag for it. If there isn't, create one. Yep, you can do that! Put the number sign (#) in front of the word or phrase you want to use and... blamo, you just created a hashtag.

Just remember not every post needs to have a link or hashtag, keep it simple.

### Inform, educate & engage by sharing links and hashtags.

# Share A Question
## SHARE #25

Posting a question is the easiest way to generate an open-ended response. It gives people free-reign to say what they want and post how they feel.

**All-Type Vacuum**
Ray Manzarek's passing brings to mind a question.....what's your favorite "Doors" tune?

**IO Creative Group**
Question of the week: Do you watch any business reality shows? If so, which one(s)?

**Cheryl A. Fuss**
What is your VERY FAVORITE LOCAL place to eat?

As you can see, it's not difficult. In fact, it's one of the most effective ways to engage friends, fans and followers through social media. Asking questions is a great way to learn how people view you, your product or service or get them to reveal their musical interests.

Asking questions will also help you find a new eatery to try out or what reality shows are worth watching.

Village Greens Golf, Inc in Strasburg PA is probably one of the finest miniature golf courses on the East Coast and here they are asking people to guess the name of a full size golf course in New Jersey. Brilliant!

 **Village Greens Golf, Inc.**
Those who have found this course located in New Jersey's lonesome Pine Barrens say it is one of the world's finest. Can you guess the name of it?

Quick, what's your favorite color?
Who won the Kentucky Derby in 1917?
Who's buried in Grant's Tomb?

Your questions are limited only by your imagination. Make it point to ask questions, it's a great way to interact with people and the answers may just surprise you. And might even give you something to laugh and smile at.

**Discover fast, funny & brilliant answers just by sharing a question.**

# Share Everything
## SHARE #26

To be honest, I'm not a big sports fan, sorry to disappoint! I don't mind playing it, just can't stand watching it on TV, listening to it on the radio or even hearing people talk about. It's just not something that appeals to me. Now if social media, or writing or even using tech stuff was a sport I would be all in...but unfortunately, what I like doesn't always jive with others.

Story of my life!

See, I just shared something else with you. How about a few more?

- I don't like okra!
- I took a belly dancing class last year with my wife so we could spend time together. Stop laughing, it was fun!
- My first job paid $3.35 an hour bagging groceries.
- The car I drove in high school was a 1974 Ford Pinto!
- I got married in 1989 and we are still together!

Hey, I did say everything, right? That's precisely why this is called, "Share Everything". It's kind of the "free for all" category. Whatever doesn't fit in the other ones, can be used here. (Well, to an extent...use common sense...if it's not something grandma would approve don't post it!)

I'm a big fan of the Chicken Soup for the Soul series but this picture from Miesse Candies says it all...

What else can you share?

How about share your Facebook page with your Twitter friends or your LinkedIn profile with your Google+ hangout buddies. Share recipes! Share vacation destinations! Share weight loss tips! Share book recommendations! Share your bad day! Share your tattoo! Share your ideas and your thoughts. Share it all!

**Share everything!**

# Share it all over again.
## SHARE #27

Yes, share it all over again! It's okay to repeat posts. In fact, I highly encourage it. You see, if you have a rather big friends list (a couple thousand) they might not have seen the message you posted the first time. And, frankly the way Facebook is aggregating their news feeds only 20% (if that) are regularly seeing what you post.

So, recycle those old posts and give them additional time to be seen.

And, if you think your friends will remember that you already shared that particular post a month ago, or six months or whenever...most likely they won't!

Heck, I've taken posts from a year ago that didn't get any likes or comments, reposted it and wham-o... people responded.

I've even reposted something I posted the week before just to remind people of the importance of my post.

Look, it could've been your timing! Maybe you

posted at an odd hour when most of your friends were sleeping and the response rate was lowered or rendered void. Or, whatever news was being shown at the time overshadowed your message.

It happens!

Twitter is a good example of why repeating posts is a good idea. The feed (or stream) is not set up like Facebook and it's more rapid, more "live" so you may not see everything going on at once. So repeating already shared posts is a fantastic way to deliver your message to the masses.

A friend of mine ran an experiment where he created a list of initially 30 posts. He shared one post per day, then repeated it the next month. Every week he would add 2 new posts to the rotation. By the end of one year he had roughly 130 repeating posts being shown. And his online business grew 57% as a result.

Share what is comfortable for you to share. Use your own good judgment. Don't force yourself to post just for the sake of getting something out. And if you don't like what you posted you can always delete it. That being said...have fun. Learn how to share and you'll be surprised at how fast you boost your social media experience, build trust and attract followers.

SHARE

# Chapter 6

# Answers Shared

# SHARE

# Getting the Most from Your Social Media Experience – FAQ's

- **What does Social Media mean to you?** *In the social media classes I've taught, the majority of attendees all said relatively the same thing...a time waster! They just didn't understand the concept of what social media could do for them or their business. They didn't understand the power of sharing.*

- **What Social Media really is?** *It comes down to one word...and if you read this book...you should be able to answer this. (Hint: it's the Title!)*

- **Will Social Media replace my current marketing?** *No! Although, I will add that when used effectively it will enhance your marketing and help you communicate better with your fans, friends and followers.*

- **What's the difference between a Facebook group page and a fanpage?** *Fanpages were designed to give profiles to businesses, celebrities or brands so they could interact with their followers. Group pages can be used the same way however, what makes group pages different is that they are more restrictive. Anyone can follow a* *fanpage, but group pages were designed to be exclusive and selective. You either ask to join or are invited to join.*

- **What is Facebook's New Graph Search?** *In a nutshell, it's a fantastic way to isolate your friends, fans and followers into specialized lists based on defined demographics.*

- **What should I post about?** *In one word...everything!*

- **What is LinkedIn?** *Think of LinkedIn as your online resource to connect you with other like minded business individuals. And your LinkedIn profile as your digital resume (on steroids). LinkedIn takes social networking to a whole different level. The connections are more valuable in a sense that you are communicating with the movers, shakers and the decision makers of the world and not some someone who is constantly posting the newest alcoholic drink they just downed or how funny their cat looks like in glasses and pajamas.*

- **Why 99% of people have their LinkedIn profile headline listed wrong?** *LinkedIn uses powerful search features to allow users to find you based on keywords. Many users make the mistake of putting their current job listing in their profile. Since your current job listing is already in your employment section why list it twice? This is redundant! Your profile is about you, your personality* and what makes you stand out. (Example: my profile – Entrepreneur, Business Coach, Marketer, SEO & Social Media Expert, Speaker, Writer & Family Man)

- **Which social media network is best?** *There is no best! Each network is designed a little differently. Twitter is great for using hashtags, LinkedIn for business contacts, Google + has hangouts and Facebook has instant chat. Using all of them increases your messages reach and allows better interaction with your followers.*

- **How frequently should I post?** *There is no set frequency...post once a week, once a day, or several times day...whatever you fancy. It's up to you. I will say this, if your goal is to build a following, posting once a week probably won't be enough. So, get into the habit of sharing at least one post a day to increase your friends, fans and followers.*

- **I'm going on vacation, but my boss wants me to still post on the business page, what do I do?** *Great question...and I can't believe you don't want to take your work with you. Just kidding. Did you ever hear the phrase, "set it and forget it"? It works for social media and it's not only a time saver, but allows you to effectively streamline your posts days, weeks and months in advance. There are many sites that allow you to do just that, but the two I recommend are Hootsuite and GrabInbox.*

SHARE

# Acknowledgements

I'd like to thank all those who allowed me to share their examples through this book. I'd like to also thank St. Philip The Apostle Catholic Church, Boy Scout Troop 24 and Boy Scouts of America Pennsylvania Dutch Council for allowing me to constantly tweak and experiment with their social media fan pages.

Gratitude goes out to all my BEN (Business & Entrepreneur Network) friends for all the great marketing ideas, Jeff Cross who has invited me to speak on social media many times, and to the many awesome people I've interviewed for my Passions to Profits audio series.

This book started out totally different. And I shelved it many times. So, I want to thank the great speakers at InfusionCon 2013 for "bragging" how easy writing a book would be. I took their advice and on the return plane home sketched out ideas for 4 books, this being one of them.

And I want to give special thanks to all my clients who shared their experience using my service with their friends and family, without your support, my business wouldn't be what it is today.

Thank you!

Rob

# About the Author

Rob Anspach is a savvy entrepreneur who just like most, struggled to find the right ways to do things, tackling projects and suffering losses that helped changed him for the better. He spent 15 years studying marketing, discovering what makes people tick, their oddities, their habits and the causes that drive them to make a purchase. Now he teaches other entrepreneurs and small & large businesses how to develop online & offline attraction mechanisms to get consumers to buy from them.

Rob has spent nearly two decades in the cleaning industry not only owning and operating a carpet cleaning business, but writing articles and teaching other cleaning entrepreneurs how to achieve success. Some of Rob's marketing pieces have appeared in Mike Capuzzi's Copy Doodles Swipe File 2011 and The Best of BEN (Business & Entrepreneur Network) Premiere Collection of Top BEN Member Marketing Campaigns & Advertising Strategies Swipe File 2012.

Rob has been a guest speaker at Jeff Cross' Totally Booked University marketing event several times, where he's spoken about using social media more effectively to gain friends, fans and followers. Some of the subjects he teaches in these marketing events include: Improving your fanpage to attract more quality followers, How to use Facebook's New Graph Search, What LinkedIn is and the right way to use it, The sneaky way to use hashtags to uncover what your competition is doing, and the Do's and Don'ts to posting to social media.

SHARE

# My Gifts To You... Absolutely <u>FREE</u>!

In this book, which I hope you read, I mention my **"Passions to Profits"** audio interview series. Well, here is where I share with you more about them and how you can get 4 of my interviews without cost or obligation of any kind... my gifts to you.

<u>Here's what you'll discover</u>

- ✓ Why offering free estimates is a waste of time.
- ✓ *How taking vacations can make you more money.*
- ✓ The importance of having mentors.
- ✓ *Why guarantees work.*
- ✓ How to use your website to qualify a customer.
- ✓ *Making time for family and hobbies.*
- ✓ What makes video so appealing.
- ✓ *How to get visitors to stay longer on your website.*
- ✓ Why firing yourself makes you more money.
- ✓ *The importance of more spokes on a wheel.*
- ✓ Why neglecting R&D could cost you.
- ✓ *Why bigger is better when it comes to social media.*
- ✓ How to develop consistent patterns.
- ✓ *How to be a world class copywriter.*
- ✓ Why storytelling is so important.

These interviews are jammed packed with over 4 hours of brilliant business building advice, tips, tricks and solutions to make you a better entrepreneur and I'm giving them to you as my gift to help you succeed.

Just go to my website... **RobAnspach.com**, sign up for my newsletter and the audio interviews will be rushed to your inbox free of charge.

# Speaking & Coaching

Whether you're looking for a speaker who uses stories and past experience to educate, entertain and engage your audience or a coach who understands what it's like to operate a business from the trenches…you need to contact Rob Anspach!

Here's what others have said about Rob…

*"If you're looking for social media or marketing advice and help, you need to be talking to Rob Anspach. Not only is Rob extremely knowledgeable, but he cares so much about every client he works with. If you're looking for help, you owe it to yourself to give Rob a call and see what he has to say…and then hire him to help you."* –Diane Conklin, Complete Marketing Systems

*"I would recommend following Rob Anspach on social media and opt-in to his email newsletter. He gives tremendous value in his willingness to share his expertise in the field of online and offline marketing. My relationship with him is invaluable."* – Andrew Mazer, ModernCoupon.com

*"Rob is as good as it gets. On time, on the mark, knows exactly what to do, and, he does it. You will not find any better."* – Terry Reiling, Reiling Automotive

**Call 1(412)ANSPACH today!**
That's 1(412)267-7224
**or visit**
**RobAnspach.com**

SHARE

# Recommended Resources

I'd like to share with you some books, seminars, websites and other resources that will help you in your quest to be a better entrepreneur.

### Recommended Reading...

"**No BS**" Series of Books by Dan S Kennedy
"**Stick Like Glue**" by Jim Palmer
"**Triggers**" by Joseph Sugarman
"**Aladdin Factor**" by Mark Victor Hansen, Jack Canfield
"**Getting Everything You Can Out Of Everything You Got**" by Jay Abraham
"**How To Sell At Prices Higher Than Your Competitors**" by Lawrence Steinmetz

### Recommended Events & Seminars...

**SuperConference** by GKIC – www.dankennedy.com
**InfusionCon** presented by InfusionSoft – www.infusioncon.com
**Business & Entrepreneurs Network** (BEN) – www.benresults.com
**Totally Booked University** – www.totallybookeduniversity.com

### Recommended Websites...

**Drew Michael Taylor Foundation** - www.drewmichaeltaylor.org
**Modern Coupon** – www.moderncoupon.com
**Cleanfax Magazine** – www.cleanfax.com
**Dulaney Cavaliers** – www.dulaneycavaliers.com
**Florida Leisure** – www.floridaleisure.com
**Lee Milteer** – www.milteer.com
**Gardners Mattress & More** – www.gardnersmattressandmore.com
**Christopher West** – www.christopherwest.com
**Miesse Candies** – www.miessecandies.com

Do you know a friend, colleague, or perhaps a group that would enjoy and benefit from this book?
If so, I'm happy to extend the following volume discounts!

## SHARE

27 Ways To Boost Your Social Media Experience, Build Trust And Attract Followers

$19.95 US

Special Quantity Discounts (subject to change)
5-25 Books - $17.95
26-50 Books - $15.95
51-100 Books - $13.95
101-250 Books - $11.95
251-500 Books - $8.95

Call or email today to order bulk quantities
(412) 267-7224
rob@robanspach.com

# #Share27Ways Photo Contest

Take a picture of you with my book and post to my FB wall www.facebook.com/robanspach1 or email it to rob@robanspach.com and you'll be entered to win a social media consultation & makeover valued at $4,995

1 winner selected every 3 months

Here's some photos of past submissions...

If you have the Kindle version take a picture with your device with the "Share" cover visible then email or post.

# Share this book!

I mean it!

Tell your friends all about this book.

Share where you bought it.

Share it at lunch!

Share it at the gym!

Share it on the beach!

Share it on social media.

Share it using this hashtag...

**#Share27Ways**


Also if you enjoy this book would do me the honor of giving me a 5 star recommendation and testimonial on www.Amazon.com , www.BN.com
or your favorite online book retailer.

Made in the USA
Lexington, KY
14 December 2019